GIANT BOOK OF
PUT-DOWNS
INSULTS
& EXCUSES!

By
JOSEPH ROSENBLOOM & MAUREEN KUSHNER

Illustrations By
SANFORD HOFFMAN & JOYCE BEHR

Main Street

10 9 8 7 6 5 4 3 2 1

Published In 1999 by Sterling Publishing Company, Inc.
387 Park Avenue South, New York, N.Y. 10016

Material in this collection was adapted from
Perfect Put-Downs and Instant Insults,
Funny Insults & Snappy Put-Downs
© Joseph Rosenbloom
and
The Funniest Excuse Book Ever
© Maureen Kushner

Distributed in Canada by Sterling Publishing
c/o Canadian Manda Group
One Atlantic Avenue, Suite 105
Toronto, Ontario, Canada M6K 3E7

Distributed in Great Britain and Europe by Chris Lloyd
463 Ashley Road, Parkstone, Poole,
Dorset, BH14 0AX, United Kingdom

Distibuted in Australia by Capricorn Link (Australia) Pty Ltd.
P.O. Box 6651, Baulkham Hills, Business Centre,
NSW 2153, Australia

Sterling ISBN 0-8069-2081-5

CONTENTS

PUT-DOWNS & INSULTS!

EXCUSES! EXCUSES!

1
FACING THE MUSIC

Hello, there—tall, dark and obnoxious!

You've really got "It"—what, I couldn't say!

I'd like to see you again—but not in person.

What you lack in modesty, you make up for in conceit.

"I'm affected?—Moi?"

Your nose is so high in the air—every time you sneeze, you spray the ceiling.

You must have trouble finding hats to fit your head. They don't make them that large.

You have such a swelled head, you have to pin back your ears to get through revolving doors.

I wish you were on TV. Then I could turn you off.

Your singing reminds me of a baseball pitcher who can't throw the ball—off pitch.

The only time your voice sounds good is when you gargle.

You sound good when you sing solo— solo no one can hear you.

I wish you'd sing Christmas carols. Then I'd only have to listen to you once a year.

I like the way you sing except for two things—my ears.

You're always forgetting things. You're for getting this, for getting that . . . .

You have a great voice. It grates on everyone.

"You remind me of the ocean."
    "Because I'm wild and romantic?"
"No, because you make me sick."

You're the kind of person who wants his cake—and everyone else's, too.

"When tourists visit your town, they go out of their way to see you."
    "Because I'm so famous?"
"No, because you're such a sight."

Is that your hair—or did you just walk through a car wash?

You have so many things on your mind, you don't have any room for brains.

Where did you get your brains—at the bird store?

Your jokes are so funny—they're greeted by tremendous bursts of silence.

The only funny lines you have are in your face.

Some people are has beens. You're a never was.

You started on the bottom—and it's been downhill ever since.

DONT' WORRY ABOUT LOSING YOUR MIND—

You weren't using it, anyway.

You're better off without it.

You'd never miss it.

Oops—it's too late!

I'VE SEEN BETTER—

I've seen better hair on coconuts.

I've seen better necks on bottles.

I've seen better tongues on sneakers.

I've seen better bodies on trucks.

I've seen better thighs on chickens.

I've seen better legs on pianos.

I've seen better teeth on a comb.

I've seen better arms on a chair.

I've seen better faces on clocks.

I'VE SEEN BETTER—

I've seen better ears on corn.

I've seen better hands on a watch.

I've seen better noses on airplanes.

I've seen better eyes on potatoes.

I've seen better heads on cabbages.

I've seen better shoulders on the side of the road.

I've seen better skin on crocodiles.

I've seen better legs on chickens.

I've seen better feet on ducks.

That was a popular song—at least, it was until you sang it.

Listen to that voice! You sound like a frog with a man in its throat.

Your voice is like asthma set to music.

You sing like a bird—a screech owl!

Your tongue may be sharp, but your voice is flat.

You have a fine voice. Don't spoil it by singing.

If baloney were snow, you'd be a blizzard.

"I played Beethoven yesterday."
 "Who won?"

You're so unpopular, you couldn't take out the garbage.

You say you can't sing because you have a hoarse throat? Well, why don't you let the horse sing? It probably has a better voice.

You're always willing to face the music—so long as you can call the tune.

You don't have a better idea—just a louder voice.

You're so boring, you couldn't even entertain a doubt.

Do you mind if I have you X-rayed? I want to see what you see in you.

You're so boring that when you go to the beach, the tide refuses to come in.

I don't mind that you're talking, so long as you don't mind that I'm not listening.

Keep talking. I always yawn when I'm interested.

You're so sick, anyone who goes out with you needs a doctor's prescription.

Some day you're going to find yourself—and wish you hadn't.

You may be beautiful from head to foot—but you're a total mess in between.

You're a real Don Juan—and I Don Juan (don't want) to have anything to do with you.

You have lovely blond hair down your back. It would look better on your head.

Your ears are cute. Too bad there's nothing in between.

People clap when they see you—their hands over their eyes!

I heard you were going to have your face lifted. But I couldn't figure out who would want to steal it.

2
WHAT'S COOKING?

Your cooking warms the heart—actually, it gives people heartburn.

Your cooking defies gravity. It's as heavy as lead, but it won't go down!

You are the garlic in the breath of life.

Tell me, what was this before you cooked it?

YOU ARE WHAT YOU EAT—

You are what you eat—
you must eat a lot of crumbs.

You are what you eat—
you must eat a lot of nuts.

You are what you eat—
you must eat a lot of garbage.

You are what you eat—
you must eat a lot of spaghetti—
you're such a meatball!

The only exercise you get is running people down, sidestepping responsibilities and putting your foot in your mouth.

You're so fat, you can only play Seek.

Whatever is eating you must be suffering horribly

THE ONLY
REGULAR EXERCISE YOU GET—

The only regular exercise you get is—
dragging your heels.

The only regular exercise you get is—
pushing your luck.

The only regular exercise you get is—
going downhill fast.

The only regular exercise you get is—
fishing for compliments.

The only regular exercise you get is—
stepping out.

The only regular exercise you get is—
driving me crazy.

The only regular exercise you get is—
running out of nachos.

When are you going to the zoo to give your face back to the monkey?

"My nose is always stuck in a book."
   "Right—you're too cheap to buy a bookmark!"

"I've got a mind of my own."
   "Good, do you think you can figure out where you left it?"

"I've changed my mind."
   "Wonderful—what did you do with the diaper?"

"I've got one of those rare minds—"
   "True—it rarely works."

The bigness of your mouth can't hide the smallness of your brain.

Arguing with you is like trying to blow out a light bulb.

Are you sure you don't work for an aspirin company? You're always giving me a headache.

Why don't you go to the library and brush up on your ignorance?

YOU'RE SO THIN—

You're so thin that when you stand sideways
in school, the teacher marks you absent.

You're so thin, the scale goes down
when you get on it.

You're so thin, you have to jump around
in the shower to get wet.

You have an inferiority complex, and it's entirely justified.

Some say you are dead when your brain stops working.
They're wrong. Your brain hasn't worked for years.

Some people are bad, but you're an exception—
exceptionally bad.

Until you came along, I never saw a prune with legs.

You're not as bad as people say—you're worse.

With the cost of living so high, why do you bother?

If I ever said anything nice about you, please cancel it.

"I feel like a piece of chocolate."
    "Well, stick around. If I get hungry I'll bite you."

"Your mind is so low—"
    "How low is it?"
"Your mind is so low that when you get a headache, you put the aspirin in your socks."

Only your red, bloodshot eyes keep you from being entirely colorless.

"I'm very fastidious."
    "Right, you're fast and you're hideous."

"I think I stripped my gears."
    "Oh, is that why you're so shiftless?"

You're a detour on the road of life.

"I'm going to buy some dog food."
    "Oh, are you ready for lunch?"

3
WHICH ONE IS THE DUMBBELL?

When you're lifting weights, it's hard to tell which one is the dumbbell.

I'm busy now. Do you mind if I ignore you some other time?

YOU'RE IN SUCH BAD SHAPE—

You're in such bad shape—
every morning you bend over and touch
your toes, with your stomach.

You're in such bad shape—
if you played the piano, the piano would win.

You're in such bad shape—
if you ran a bath, you'd come in second.

You're in such bad shape—
if you beat an egg, we'd all be surprised.

You're in such bad shape—
the only muscles (mussels) you've got
are still in the shell.

YOU'RE IN SUCH BAD SHAPE—

You're in such bad shape—
you couldn't even catch your breath.

You're in such bad shape—
you couldn't even crack a joke.

You're in such bad shape—
when you sit down you look like batter spreading.

You're in such bad shape—
when you sip lemonade, you have to hold
onto your chair to keep from getting
sucked back into the straw.

You're in such bad shape—
you couldn't even beat a drum.

Who am I calling stupid? I don't know—what's your name?

You used to have a decent build before your stomach went in for a career of its own.

You look fit as a fiddle—a bull fiddle.

Did you hear the jokes about your muscles? Never mind— they're a lot of mush.

What makes you think you're in bad shape— just ignore the buzzards flying overheard!

I'm out of shape? You're jello with a belt!

You're in shape all right— the wrong shape!

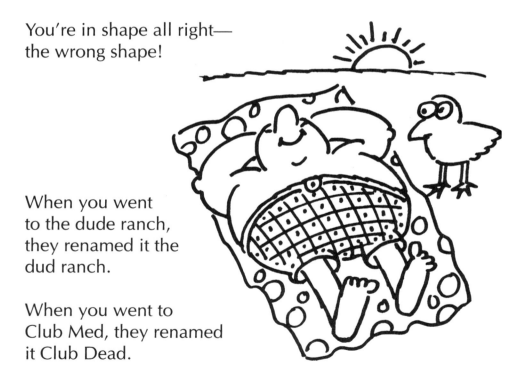

When you went to the dude ranch, they renamed it the dud ranch.

When you went to Club Med, they renamed it Club Dead.

JUST BECAUSE

Just because you have athlete's foot
doesn't make you an athlete.

Just because you're teed off all the time
doesn't make you a golfer.

Just because you were thrown out at home
doesn't make you a baseball player.

Just because you've been left back
doesn't make you a football player.

Just because you make a racket
doesn't make you a tennis player.

Your head reminds me of a bowling ball—it's hard, round and has holes in it.

You remind me of racquetball—off the wall.

The only thing fast about you is your watch.

YOU'RE SO DUMB—

You're so dumb—
you would try to shake hands with a palm tree.

You're so dumb—
you think the Kentucky Derby is a hat.

You're so dumb—
if you went to buy a color TV set,
you wouldn't know what color to get.

You're so dumb—
I hear you took your nose apart to find out
what made it run.

You're so dumb—
I hear you put your watch in the piggy bank
so you could save time.

I used to think turtles were slow—until I saw you running.

The only running you have anything to do with is reruns on TV.

You, a jogger? The only thing that runs around your house is the fence!

Your feet are so big, you don't need skis to go water skiing.

Now I know reincarnation is a fact. No one could possibly get as stupid as you are in just one lifetime.

You must have been hit on the head with a baseball bat when you were a baby, because you've been off base ever since.

Your mouth is getting too big for your muzzle.

You remind me of Plymouth Rock. You have a shape like a Plymouth and a head like a rock.

You're a lost treasure. How I wish you'd stay lost!

If you have to fall, fall on your head. You can't get hurt that way.

"I'm so strong, I can bend bars!"
    "Sure, chocolate bars."

You're strong as an ox and almost as intelligent.

4
YOU MOVED!

You're pretty as a picture—and you should be hung.

I heard you were at the dog show. Who won second prize?

You're certainly shipshape—shaped like a ship.

You waited so long for your dreamboat to come in, your pier collapsed.

You have what it takes—but you've had it so long, it's gone bad.

Your stomach is so big that when you get your shoes shined, you have to take the man's word for it.

You're an all-around person—especially around the middle.

You're so fat, you're the same size whether you stand up or sit down.

You weigh so much, when you get into a rowboat, it becomes a submarine.

Fat? You must have a truck scale in your bathroom.

What time is it when you get on a scale? Time to get a new scale!

YOU'RE SUCH A BAD ARTIST—

You're such a bad artist—
you couldn't even draw your breath.

You're such a bad artist—
you couldn't even draw the curtains.

You're such a bad artist—
you couldn't even draw a bath.

You're such a bad artist—
you couldn't even draw the shade.

You're such a bad artist—
you couldn't even draw a sword.

You're such a bad artist—
you couldn't even draw a salary.

You once had wavy hair—
but one day it waved goodbye.

I hear you read a book—once.

Time marches on, why
don't you?

Of course you're not bald.
It's just that the part in your hair
covers your whole head.

You still chase girls—but only downhill.

You ring my chimes. No wonder—you're a real ding-a-ling.

Greedy? You're a human gimmee pig.

No wonder you have headaches. Your ignorance is
crowding out what's left of your brains.

Just because everyone gives you the brush-off doesn't make
you a great painter.

You ought to be a geologist—you have rocks in your head.

You ought to be a geologist—you have so many faults.

"My throat is hoarse."
    "The rest of you looks that way, too."

You have a waterproof voice. Nothing can drown it out.

THEY ALL MUST LOVE YOU—

Lawyers must love you—
you're such a case.

Ventriloquists must love you—
you're such a dummy.

Birdwatchers must love you—
you're so featherbrained.

Brooks must love you—
you never stop babbling.

Eye doctors must love you—
you're always making a spectacle of yourself.

Soldiers must love you—
you're always shooting your mouth off.

You have two ears and one tongue, so why don't you listen twice as much as you talk?

Your mouth reminds me of a car without brakes. It can't be stopped.

You have the manners of a gentleman. Either start using them or give them back!

Your idea of cleaning a room is to sweep it with a glance.

You can help me clean my house. I'd like to mop up the floor with you.

Your home is free of mice and cockroaches. They refuse to live in the same place as you.

You used to be arrogant and obnoxious, but now you're just the opposite. Now you're obnoxious and arrogant.

You're like a slow leak. People can hear you, but they can't turn you off.

Your mouth may be fresh, but your ideas are stale.

I can always tell when you're lying—your lips are moving.

You always tell the truth—if it's more convenient.

You always tell the truth—but only after you've run out of lies.

You're a free thinker. Your ideas aren't worth anything.

Anyone who offered you a penny for your thoughts would be overpaying.

"My boyfriend says I'm a peach."
　　"That's because you have a heart of stone."

If you need me, don't hesitate to ask—someone else!

You grow on people—like a wart.

5
COME OUT FIGHTING!

You'll be a great fighter—Your breath would knock anyone out

You may be down to earth, but not far enough down to suit me.

You have a mechanical mind. Too bad all the parts are rusted.

No one can get close to you when you're talking. The blast of hot air drives everyone back.

The only way you can get a hot idea is to stick your head in the oven.

A thought struck you once, and you've been unconscious ever since.

The last time a thought struck you, the experience was so painful, you decided never to let it happen again.

You don't know whether you're coming or going—you must bump into yourself a lot.

Here's a lighted dynamite stick. Please hold it for me till I get back.

Would you mind reaching into your head and getting me a handful of sawdust?

Your breath is so bad, you have to use industrial strength mouthwash.

I wish you'd lose your temper. The one you have now is awful.

When you graduated from school, they gave you a no-class ring.

THEY ALL MUST LOVE YOU—

Bowlers must love you—
you have a pin head.

Basketball players must love you—
you dribble all over yourself.

Tennis players must love you—
they love nothing.

Baseball players must love you—
you're always out in left field.

Balloonists must love you—
you're so full of hot air.

Race car drivers must love you—
you're always trying to pull a fast one.

You have a mechanical mind. Too bad the gears are stripped.

You have a mind like half a dictionary—it never gets to "Think."

If you were twice as smart, you'd still be stupid.

Of course you don't have an inferiority complex. You're too simple to have any complex.

You're like two tailors who need a bath—a dirty sew-and-sew.

You remind me of a magician who never takes a bath, always up to dirty tricks.

Where did you learn to fight—at Kentuckey Fried Chicken?

You're like a phonograph record. You go round and round, but never get anywhere.

When can you spell idiot in one letter? When it's "U."

"I'm nobody's fool."
   "Too bad—maybe somebody will adopt you."

You're a square shooter—one of those squares I'd like to shoot.

You come from such a crooked family, even your inlaws are outlaws.

People like you are like pearls—they need to be strung up.

The only thing about you that's on the level is your flat head.

The hardness of your head is made up for by the softness of your brain.

Your head is so flat, flies use it for a landing field.

What did your right ear say to your left ear?
    "Do you live on this block, too?"

THE ONLY TIME—

The only time you have a heart
is when you're playing cards.

The only time you have charms
is when you wear a bracelet.

The only time you have appeal
is when you're eating a banana.

6
MONKEYING AROUND

I've had a wonderful time—but this isn't it.

I may be a jogger and you may be a jogger, but there's no way I'd ever run around with you.

The only way I could be stuck on you is with a stapler.

The only way I'd go around with you is if we were stuck in the same revolving door.

The only kind of kisses you'll ever get from me is the chocolate kind.

"At night when I'm asleep, into my dreams you creep. In fact, you're the biggest creep I ever met!"

The only kind of date you can get is off a calendar.

You have an even disposition—always rotten.

"I feel like a sandwich."
    "Funny, you look more like a marshmallow to me."

You're a real big gun—of small caliber and a big bore.

You have a wonderful face. One look and people wonder.

Your face isn't a horror—it's a scream.

Your face looks like mashed potatoes, with the lumps still in them.

You don't need luggage when you travel. You have enough bags under your eyes.

Did you hear the joke about your complexion? Never mind, I don't tell off-color stories.

Help reduce air pollution—stop breathing!

YOU'RE SO REPULSIVE—

You're so repulsive—
even a magnet wouldn't be attracted to you.

You're so repulsive—
even the ocean wouldn't wave when it saw you.

You're so repulsive—
even a clock wouldn't give you the time of day.

You're so repulsive—
even a boomerang wouldn't come back to you.

You're so repulsive—
even a bee wouldn't buzz you.

You're so repulsive—
even an echo wouldn't call you back.

If you played hide-and-seek, no one would bother to look for you.

Give you an inch and you think you're a ruler.

There are three kinds of people: those who make things happen, those who watch things happen—and people like you, who wonder what happened.

You have such a dirty mind, you better shampoo with deodorant.

You remind me of shampoo—the way you're always getting in everyone's hair.

Your head is like a doorknob—anyone can turn it.

You don't wear lipstick. You can't keep your mouth closed long enough to put it on.

YOU REMIND ME—

You remind me of a tiny deck of cards—
you're no big deal.

You remind me of a school without a head—
you lack principles.

You remind me of a school without teachers—
you've lost your faculties.

You remind me of a movie star—
Boris Karloff.

You remind me of an old pair of shoes—
a lowdown heel with no sole.

You remind me of a whale—
always spouting off.

You remind me of a flower—
you lilac crazy.

YOU REMIND ME—

You remind me of a broom—
anyone can shove you around.

You remind me of an amoeba—
you're a lower form of life.

You remind me of a postage stamp—
anyone can lick you.

You remind me of a movie star—
Lassie.

You remind me of oatmeal—
lukewarm and mushy.

You remind me of a watermelon—
pitiful.

You remind me of a yo-yo—
you're such a jerk.

YOU REMIND ME—

You remind me of a fat man's button—
always popping off at the wrong time.

You remind me of a broken zipper—
always stuck and off the track.

You remind me of an unframed picture—
off the wall.

You remind me of a sidewalk sale—
50% off.

You remind me of a bag of pistachios—
totally nuts.

You remind me of a saint—
a Saint Bernard.

You remind me of a canoe—
you behave better when paddled from the rear.

You're a very modest person, and you have lots to be modest about.

The only polish you have is on your nails.

The only polish you'll ever have is on your shoes.

When I see two people together and one looks bored, the other one is you.

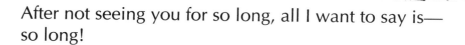

You're one in a million—thank goodness!

After not seeing you for so long, all I want to say is—so long!

7
THE LATEST DOPE

What's the latest dope—besides you?

The sharpness of your tongue is only exceeded by the dullness of your mind.

You talk twice as fast as anyone can listen.

JUST BECAUSE

Just because you're all wrapped up in yourself
doesn't make you a prize package.

Just because you step all over people
doesn't mean you're getting up in the world.

Just because you have legs like a canary
doesn't mean you're a singer.

Just because you're a million years old and gassy
doesn't make you a star.

Just because you go from the
frying pan into the fire
doesn't make you hot stuff.

Just because your head is shaped like a hubcap
doesn't make you a big wheel.

Just because you're a son of a gun
doesn't make you a big shot.

May I have your picture?
I need it for my dart board.

You must be a terrible bowler. Your mind is always in the gutter.

"I have a dynamic personality."
    "Yes, and it's underwhelming!"

You're so loud, you even whisper at the top of your voice.

You remind me of last week's newspaper—stale, unimportant, and filled with bad news.

You have the germ of an idea. Please don't spread it around.

"I passed your house yesterday."
    "Thanks awfully!"

Why do you take yourself so seriously? No one else does.

The only way you'll ever get a fine finish is to drink shellac.

Anyone who told you to be yourself couldn't have given you worse advice.

How much would you charge to haunt a house?

You're such a big nothing, you have to rent a shadow.

You're such a big nothing that when you get into a taxi, the driver keeps the "Vacant" sign up.

I hear the president is going to declare you a national disaster area.

I hear you flunked out of dog obedience school. You couldn't keep up with the rest of the class.

THEY ALL MUST LOVE YOU—

Farmers must love you—
you're always making a pig of yourself.

Pigs must love you—
you're such a ham.

Coffee makers must love you—
you're an automatic drip.

Maple trees must love you—
you're such a sap.

Bakers must love you—
you're such a fruitcake.

Knife sharpeners must love you—
you're so dull.

It's great to have brains. But then again, how would you know?

You have rare ideas. It's rare when you have any.

You're so full of ignorance, it's coming out of your mouth.

You think you're sharp as a tack, but you're only tacky.

You approach every subject with an open mouth.

Do you know how to improve your speech? Use shortening.

Every time you open your mouth, some idiot starts talking.

Even an owl wouldn't give a hoot for you.

You may go around in circles, but you're still a square.

There are two sides to every question—your side and the truth.

"Did you hear the joke about the moron who kept on saying no?"
   "No."
"So you're the one!"

Your jokes are from Poland—they get Warsaw and Warsaw.

The closest you'll ever come to being a joker is to find one in a deck of cards.

Be careful you don't break your arm patting yourself on the back.

Let's play horse. I'll be the front end, and you just be yourself.

Your conversation is so dull,
you won't even talk to yourself.

You're such a hog, pigs must follow
you around!

Do skunks come up to you and ask you how you do it?

Half of your jokes are witty. No wonder you're a half-wit.

I'll never forget the first time I met you—but I'll keep trying.

As the painter said to the wall, "One more crack like that
and I'll plaster you!"

I am here with an open mind, a complete lack of prejudice
and a cool approach to hear the rubbish you are about to
tell me.

People like you who think they know everything are
annoying to those of us who do.

You irk me. In fact, you're the biggest irk I know.

I used to think there was no such thing as a perpetual
motion machine until I saw your mouth in action.

You're like the Invisible Man—nothing to look at.

You croak like a frog—and I wish you would!

8
PLAYING HOOKY

You think you're an actor, but the only thing you can play is hooky.

You're the only person I know who got a D in recess.

JUST BECAUSE

Just because you give everybody heartburn
doesn't mean you're so hot.

Just because you tell everybody where to go
doesn't make you a travel agent.

Just because you tell people where to get off
doesn't make you a bus driver.

Just because you're always in a jam
doesn't mean you're well preserved.

Just because you know all the angles
doesn't mean you know geometry.

Just because you smell bad
doesn't make you a big cheese.

Just because you're always in the soup
doesn't mean you've got a good noodle.

You'd be better off if you had more bone in the spine and less in the head.

You're a big pill—hard to take and tough to swallow.

You think you're a big wheel, but you're only a flat tire.

You're like time off from school—no class.

I know you're not the worst person in the world, but until a worse one comes along—you'll do.

You're in a class by yourself—no wonder, no one wants to sit next to you.

You were different from the other five-year-olds in your kindergarten class. You were twelve.

THEY ALL MUST LOVE YOU—

Ghosts must love you—
 you're such a fright.

Vampires must love you—
 you're such a pain in the neck.

Mummies must love you—
you're so wrapped up in yourself.

Skeletons must love you—
 you're such a bonehead.

Dracula must love you—
 you're such a sucker.

Extraterrestrials must love you—
 you're no earthly good.

When you were promoted from kindergarten, you were so excited, you cut yourself shaving.

You were in the same grade so long, people began to think you were the teacher.

It was a great day when you graduated. The teachers cried for joy—they thought they'd never get rid of you.

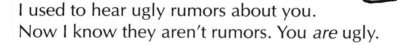

I used to hear ugly rumors about you. Now I know they aren't rumors. You *are* ugly.

The only first class thing about you is some of the mail you get.

I can live without air for minutes, without water for days, without food for weeks, and without you—forever!

The world is made up of all kinds of people: the lower crust, the upper crust, and people like you—just crust.

I used to think you were a big pain in the neck. Now I have a much lower opinion of you.

If you changed, it would have to be an improvement. You couldn't get any worse.

Your brain is a miracle—it's a miracle when it works!

Everyone has a right to be stupid—but you abuse the privilege.

You couldn't be as stupid as you look. Stupidity doesn't come in that size!

Before you become a blood donor, make sure you're a blood owner.

"I'm going to the blood bank."
   "Overdrawn again?"

Dracula would turn you down.
He wants blood, not crud.

Your nose is so big, you only
have to breathe in once and
it lasts all day.

Is that your nose—
or are you wearing a tomato?

Is that your nose—
or are you minding it for an elephant?

I was going to buy some handkerchiefs for your birthday,
but I couldn't find any big enough for your nose.

In the medical books, where they describe a moron, they
mention you as a perfect example.

No one can resist you. Your breath is enough to make
anyone cave in.

"How many ribs are there on a jackass?"
    "Open your shirt and we'll find out."

"How many hairs are there on a pig's head?"
    "Next time you use a comb, count them."

"How many toes are on a monkey's foot?"
    "Take off your shoes and let's see."

When you say, "I'm a monkey's uncle!", you must be
talking about your family.

You really use your head—to keep the rain off your neck!

I've heard of large chickens, but you're the biggest cluck I've ever seen!

Your mouth is like a chicken— foul!

There's a bus leaving in five minutes. Why don't you get under it?

9
WHERE HAVE YOU BEEN ALL MY LIFE?

Where have I been all
your life?
Mostly avoiding you.

Have you seen me someplace before?
It's possible. I've been someplace before.

Have you seen me someplace else?
Yes—and how I wish I were there now.

You're so cold-blooded, if Dracula bit you he'd get pneumonia.

I think of your personality several times every day—each time I open the refrigerator.

You not only don't know what's up—you don't know what's down or sideways.

You have what it takes. Better give it back before the police catch up with you.

IF I GAVE YOU—

If I gave you an ax—would you split?

If I gave you a drum—would you beat it?

If I gave you a pogo stick—would you hop it?

If I gave you a rubber band—would you snap out of it?

If I gave you a rope—would you skip it?

If I gave you a parachute—would you drop out?

If I gave you an airline ticket—would you take off?

If I gave you scissors—would you cut out?

If I gave you a scale—would you go weigh?

It was love at first sight. Then I took another look.

I see you're dressing formally today. You're wearing a clean shirt.

There was something about you I liked, but you spent it.

You believe in give-and-take relationships—so long as I'm the one that gives and you're the one that takes.

If your dress were cut any lower, you wouldn't need socks.

If your dress were any shorter, it would be a collar.

"You're such a pretty girl."
    "Thanks. Of course you'd say that, even if you didn't think it."
"Of course, and you'd think it even if I didn't say it."

You're like sugar—pale, lumpy and shapeless.

You have quite a figure. No one can quite figure it out.

I'd like to have the pleasure of this dance, so please dance with someone else.

When the phone rings, people hope it isn't you.

THAT LAST JOKE—

That last joke of yours was like
chicken feed—strictly for the birds.

That last joke of yours was about as funny as
a helicopter with an ejection seat.

That last joke of yours was like
a bunch of fleas—gone to the dogs.

That last joke of yours was like
last week's bread—stale.

That last joke of yours was
two-thirds of a pun—PU.

You're dark and handsome. The darker it is, the handsomer
you look.

You've been turned down more often than a bed.

WHY DON'T YOU MAKE LIKE—

Why don't you make like an egg
and get cracking?

Why don't you make like an insect
and bug off?

Why don't you make like a boat
and shove off?

Why don't you make like the wind
and blow?

Why don't you make like a curtain
and pull yourself together?

Why don't you make like a rocket
and blast off?

Why don't you make like an actor
and bow out?

I don't mind you hanging around my house. I just don't want you coming inside.

You must have gotten up on the wrong side of your cage this morning.

You're so full of hot air, you have to be careful not to start forest fires by breathing the wrong way.

You could put out forest fires all by yourself. You're a total wet blanket.

The only place you can dig up a date is in the cemetery.

All you have to do to lose ten pounds is to take a bath.

Your idea of an exciting evening is a sight-seeing trip through a garbage dump.

You're the salt of the earth. No wonder your kisses taste so awful.

Haven't you ever wondered why people close their eyes when they kiss you?

Your idea of an exciting evening is to turn up the electric blanket.

I would die for you, but mine is an undying love.

The only time you wash your ears is when you eat watermelon.

You looked everywhere and finally found someone worthy of your love—you!

"I'd go to the ends of the earth for you."
    "Yes—but would you stay there?"

How can I leave you? By bus, taxi, subway, airplane or on foot.

Don't go away mad—just go away!

10
MOTHER NATURE'S BIGGEST MISTAKE

How is Mother Nature's biggest mistake today?

"That man is following me. I think he's crazy."
   "I think so, too."

There are three sexes: male, female—and you.

A day without you is like a day with sunshine.

You look like lemon tastes.

"I'm unattached."
 "No, I think you're just put together sloppily."

I don't think you're pretty and I don't think you're ugly.
I think you're pretty ugly.

You may be a beautiful person on the inside. Too bad it's the outside that shows.

Would you like to see what a creature from outer space looks like?
Here's a mirror.

THEY ALL MUST LOVE YOU—

Tow truck drivers must love you—
you're such a wreck.

Florists must love you—
you're such a blooming idiot.

Undertakers must love you—
you're dead on your feet.

Pencil sharpeners must love you—
everything you say is pointless.

Exterminators must love you—
you're such a big pest.

Plumbers must love you—
you're such a big drip.

"I went to beauty school."
    "Couldn't pass the physical?"

"I went to charm school."
    "Flunked out?"

Your face reminds me of a relief map. It's a relief when I don't have to look at it.

"You look like a cross between Oliver Twist and David Copperfield."
    "Like a cute young kid?"
"No—like the Dickens."

You spend so much time hunting for food in the refrigerator, your nose suffers from frostbite.

WANT TO IMPROVE YOUR LOOKS?

Want to improve your looks?
    Walk backwards.

Want to improve your looks?
    Pay someone normal
        to say he's you.

Want to improve your looks?
Wear a hat—right over your face.

If it weren't for your pot belly, you'd have no shape at all.

"You look like a million dollars."
    "Don't kid me. You never saw a million dollars."
"You're right. You look like nothing I ever saw."

You went on a crash diet? No wonder you look like such a wreck!

Of course, you're not fat—you're just tall around the waist.

"My hands are soft because I wear gloves at night."
    "You must also sleep with a hat on."

The way you dress, you could enter the Mess America contest.

This is the first time I've seen a burlap bag with sleeves.

Your clothing fits like a glove. It sticks out in five places.

You're a regular clotheshorse. Your clothing would look better on a horse.

You talk so much, you must have been vaccinated with a phonograph needle.

You talk so much, your mouth needs a 50,000-mile check-up every month.

Your mind may be permanently closed, but your mouth is permanently open.

Until I met you, I thought the Mississippi had a big mouth.

You're not outspoken. No one can outspeak *you*.

Your mouth is always going—so why don't you?

YOU'RE SO OLD—

You're so old—
the birthday candles cost more than the cake.

You're so old—
by the time you light the last
birthday candles, the
first ones are out.

You're so old—
that when you went to school,
history was current
events.

Old? There were so many candles on your birthday cake, the ceiling was barbecued!

You should wear a sign on your head—HELP WANTED.

If you went to a mind reader, you'd get your money back.

You may be slow-witted, but you're fast-tongued.

The only way you can make up your mind is to put lipstick on your forehead.

I hope you have unemployment insurance for your brain. It hasn't worked since I've known you.

There is a cure for your lack of brains. It's called "silence."

Your face has more wrinkles than an accordian.

You must be at least thirty years old. I counted the rings under your eyes.

With your varicose veins, you could go to the masquerade party as a road map.

The only thing that would whistle at you is a teapot.

Some people have an inferiority complex. You have an interfere-iority complex.

You belong to the meddle class.

JUST BECAUSE—

Just because you have a short fuse
doesn't make you dynamite.

Just because you're always flying off the handle
doesn't make you a pilot.

Just because you can switch on an electric light
doesn't make you a live wire.

Just because your head comes to a point
doesn't make you real sharp.

Just because your nose runs a lot
doesn't make you a jogger.

"I'm going now. Don't trouble to see me to the door."
"No trouble—it's a pleasure!"

Germs avoid you. They don't want to get sick.

Maybe you'd be okay once I got to know you. But I don't want to take the chance.

You're so pale, if you wanted to blush, you'd have to get a blood transfusion.

Any mosquito that bit you would lose blood.

11
WHAT A PILL!

"Doctor, doctor, I feel like a cup of coffee!"
"Oh, perk up, and don't be a drip!"

"Doctor, doctor, nobody likes me!"
"Why do you think that, you boring little creep?"

THE LAST TIME I SAW
SOMETHING LIKE YOU—

The last time I saw something like you—
I took two aspirins and called the doctor.

The last time I saw something like you—
I checked into the hospital to have
my eyes examined.

The last time I saw something like you—
I threw it a bone.

The last time I saw something like you—
the undertaker was embalming it.

The last time I saw something like you—
it was swinging from a tree and eating a banana.

The last time I saw something like you—
it had three shiny leaves and a red stem—
and I didn't want to touch that, either.

"Doctor, doctor, there's a man at the door with a hideous face!"

"Tell him you already have one."

What's on your mind besides your toupee?

Your mind is first rank. It's rank, all right.

Did you hear the joke about your mind? Forget it, I don't tell dirty stories.

I was going to tell you a joke about how to lose your mind, but I see you heard it already.

They should hang a sign over your head—OUT OF ORDER.

Sit down and give your mind a rest.

If you had a brain transplant, the brain would reject *you.*

When they made you, they broke the mold. It was too moldy.

You're like a greasy deck of cards—impossible to deal with.

If you ate your words, you'd have to get your stomach pumped.

In your case, a brain operation would only be minor surgery.

If you said what was on your mind, you'd be speechless!

"Let's talk about your good points. That doesn't give us much to talk about, does it?"

Your mind is sharp as a marble.

Your problem is that you were born upside down. Your nose runs and your feet smell.

Until I heard you speak, I thought water was colorless.

You should go into show business.
You would make a great dummy
in a ventriloquist act.

You think *you* have problems—I have to listen to you!

THEY ALL MUST LOVE YOU—

Squirrels must love you—
you're such a big nut.

Caterpillars must love you—
you're such a total creep.

Fishes must love you—
you're all wet.

Owls must love you—
you never give a hoot.

Pet owners must love you—
you've gone to the dogs.

Cows must love you—
you're so moo-dy.

Before burdening other people with your troubles, remember:

Half the people you tell aren't interested in the least, and the other half are delighted that you're finally getting what you deserve.

You're very knowledgeable.
You can bore people
on any subject.

You remind me of a broken pencil sharpener. You go around in circles and never get to the point.

"Can you solve a problem for me?"
    "I'll try."
"Take one sack of sawdust, two bales of hay, and two hundred cotton balls. . . Have you got that all in your head?"
    "Yes."
"I thought so!"

Your family couldn't afford a dog. They had you instead.

I understand you were an only child. Thank goodness!

Most babies are a bundle from heaven. You're a bungle from heaven.

When you were born, your parents were hoping for a prize. Instead, they got a surprise.

You were a war baby. Your parents took one look at you and started fighting.

You were such an ugly baby, they didn't know which end to diaper.

I've heard better ideas from my parrot.

"I like to do one thing at a time."
  "So that's why your brain stops working the minute
  you open your mouth!"

One of us is crazy, but don't worry—I'll keep your secret.

You don't have to be crazy to know you, but it helps!

You haven't been yourself lately. If only you'd stay that way.

I've had many pleasant hours of restful sleep listening to you.

Why don't you go away somewhere and play with your
mental blocks?

Here's a handkerchief. Now—blow!

12

BAH, HUMBUG!

You should take up the study of space. You have the head for it.

Your presence makes me long for your absence.

The hardness of your heart is only exceeded by the softness of your muscles.

You are the missing tooth in the smile of Happiness.

You're something else—what, I'd rather not say.

You're the "tilt" in the game of Life.

Your unimportance is only matched by your insignificance.

You remind me of a seat in church—pew!

If they put your picture on a stamp, no one would lick it.

People don't need air conditioners with you around. You leave everyone cold.

You're like poison—people can't take you even in tiny doses.

Does the U.N. realize that the most underdeveloped place in the world is your brain?

You'd be better off if you lost your head. Why carry around all that dead weight?

There is one thing I'll say for you—you won't get any stupider. You couldn't.

Please don't come any closer. I'm allergic to ignorance.

The closest you'll ever come to a brainstorm is a slow drip.

If brains were dynamite, you wouldn't have enough to blow your nose.

When brains were handed out, you weren't even on line.

You must think you're in the watch business. Whenever I work—you watch.

Your shoes match your personality. Both are loafers.

You don't know the meaning
of the word "work."
You're too lazy to look it up.

You're fascinated by work. You can sit and stare at it all day.

They say work never killed anyone, but you don't want to be the first one to find out for sure.

You never open your mouth without subtracting from the sum of human knowledge.

Your ideas are like peaches—fuzzy on the outside, mushy on the inside.

You're so stingy, the only thing you'll share with anyone is measles.

You remind me of a canary—cheap! cheap!

You're a real lamb. Ask you for anything and you say, "Baaaah!"

YOU'RE SO CHEAP—

You're so cheap—
you go into a drugstore and buy one Kleenex.

You're so cheap—
when your girlfriend wanted something with
diamonds, you bought her a deck of cards.

You're so cheap—
all a pickpocket can get out of you is practice.

You're so cheap—
the only ring you ever give anyone is
a collect phone call.

You're so cheap—
you won't even pay anyone a compliment.

You're so cheap—
you won't even pay attention!

Tight? You have a one-way pocket.

You remind me of a dentist. Getting anything out of you is like pulling teeth.

Your idea of free speech is being able to use someone else's phone.

You're so short, you have to stand on a chair to brush your teeth.

You're so short, you're smaller standing up than when you're lying down.

If you have your life to live over again—please do it on another planet!

The only possible way you could ever get ahead—is to borrow one.

You're so lazy that if opportunity knocked, you'd complain about the noise.

You're so lazy, you only go through a revolving door on someone else's push.

Slow? If you were any slower, you'd be dead.

Who says doing nothing is impossible? You've been doing it all your life.

I don't know what I'd do without you—but I'd like to give it a try.

The only possible way you could get up in the world is to take an elevator.

What's your ambition in life— besides breathing?

The sooner I never see you again, the better!

13

GO TO YOUR CAGE!

People know of you by word of mouth—yours.

You're a sight for sore eyes—a real eyesore!

I wish you would get lost some place where they have no "found" department.

You must use gunpowder on your face. It looks shot.

Your mouth is like a mailbox—open day and night.

You've heard of permanent press. Well, what you're wearing looks like permanent mess.

I can read you like a book. How I wish I could shut you up like one!

You look like a million—every day of it.

One more wrinkle and you could pass for a prune.

So! That's what a mummy looks like without bandages!

You have what it takes. The only trouble is you've had it too long.

Is that your face, or are you wearing a ski mask?

You could talk your head off and never miss it.

If you had to eat your words, you'd get ptomaine poisoning.

A stocking over your face would look better than over your legs.

You couldn't be two-faced or you wouldn't be wearing the one you have on now.

I hear you were going to have your face lifted, but when you found out the price—you let the whole thing drop.

Your mind needs changing. It's filthy.

The last time I saw someone like you, I had to pay admission.

With friends like you, who needs enemies?

The only time you had a figure was when you had the mumps.

You look wonderful. Who is your embalmer?

I've never seen your tongue. It moves too fast.

The closest you'll ever get to becoming the toast of the town is a sunburn.

If you stopped using dirty words, you'd have nothing to say.

Just because you're a nag doesn't mean you have horse sense.

I hear you're not allowed to visit the zoo. Your face scares the animals.

Your outfit fits you like a glove—a catcher's mitt.

You're so neat—not a wrinkle out of place.

I've seen nicer hair on mops.

You look like a million dollars— all green and wrinkled.

Time may heal a lot of things, but it hasn't done you much good.

Your face is so wrinkled, you should have it pressed.

You remind me of history—always repeating yourself.

You're a real bargain—50% off.

No wonder you have headaches. Your halo is on too tight.

If anyone said hello to you—you'd be stuck for an answer.

The day you were born you
   cried like a baby. So did your
      parents.

Anybody who said he was crazy
   about you—would have to be.

Tell me, do you sleep with your face in the
   pillow to be kind to burglars?

You'd leave your head in bed in the
   morning if it weren't attached
      to your neck.

Why don't you hop on your
broom and fly away?

14

SHALL WE FENCE?

My doctor told me
to exercise with dumbbells.
Shall we fence?

I wouldn't say you're
a perfect idiot.
No one is perfect.

I know I am talking like
an idiot. I have to talk that
way so you can understand me.

The sharpest thing about you
is your tongue.

Keep your mouth shut.
My plants are wilting.

You may not be light on your feet, but you certainly are
light in your head.

Until I met you, I thought blood was thicker than water.

You remind me of a one-story building—nothing upstairs.

If you were a building, you'd be condemned.

You couldn't be as stupid as you look—and live.

The trouble with you is that you're forgotten—but not gone.

Why don't you put an egg in your shoe and beat it?

You shouldn't have trouble falling asleep. You're unconscious most of the time anyway.

You don't have an inferiority complex. You're just inferior.

Some people have savoir faire. You don't even have carfare.

You must have a sixth sense. There's no sign of the other five.

A thought struck you once—you were in the hospital for a month.

You remind me of a jigsaw puzzle—so many of the pieces are missing.

You're good-looking in a way—away off.

You seem to have plenty of get-up-and-go. So, why don't you?

Could I drop you off somewhere—say, the roof?

It was nice visiting your neighborhood. I enjoy slumming.

Just because you go around in circles doesn't make you a big wheel.

I know why you never go on a vacation. You're always on an ego trip.

You have only two faults—everything you do and everything you say.

If you have your life to do over again—don't!

I never forget a face, and in your case, I'll remember both of them.

You must be crazy, not because you talk to yourself, but because you listen.

If I gave you an eraser, would you rub yourself out?

Why don't you go out and play in the traffic?

You are the most complete nothing since the invention of the zero.

Would you mind closing the door—from the outside?

If you went to the zoo, people would try to feed you.

You can go back home now. They finished cleaning your cage.

Is that your face or are you breaking it in for a bulldog?

I'd like to help you out. Which way did you come in?

15
HOCUS POCUS

Did I miss you when you were gone? I didn't know you were gone.

Give me time. I'll find a way of ignoring you.

I expect you to go places—and the sooner the better.

People like you don't grow on trees—they swing from them.

You must get up early. How else could you say so many stupid things in one day?

I can depend on you. You're always around when you need me.

For a minute I thought you were crazy. I was wrong. You've been crazy for much longer than that.

I came to see you off—and you certainly are.

You're a regular information bureau—always telling people where to go.

You've given me something to live for—revenge.

One of us is crazy. But don't worry, I'll keep your secret.

You remind me of a goat—always butting in.

You should go to Hollywood. The walk will do you good.

How can I miss you if you won't go away?

If you lived by your wits, you'd starve.

They say there's a fuel shortage, but you're the biggest fuel (fool) I've ever seen.

You have a mechanical mind. Too bad so many of the screws are missing.

Keep this under your hat. I know you've got plenty of room there.

You never change your mind. You flush it.

I hear you had to drop out of kindergarten—couldn't keep up with the work.

You have a baby face—and a mind to match.

Anyone who looks like you ought to be arrested for disturbing the peace.

You're nasty, disagreeable, stupid, repulsive, obnoxious— and those are your good points.

Something is preying on your mind. But don't worry, it will soon die of starvation.

Please don't talk when I'm interrupting.

Why don't you cross the street blindfolded?

You have such a swelled head, you must have your hats made in a tent factory.

Why don't you rub vanishing cream all over yourself and disappear?

Why don't you make like a pack of cards and shuffle off?

16
DISORDER IN THE COURT

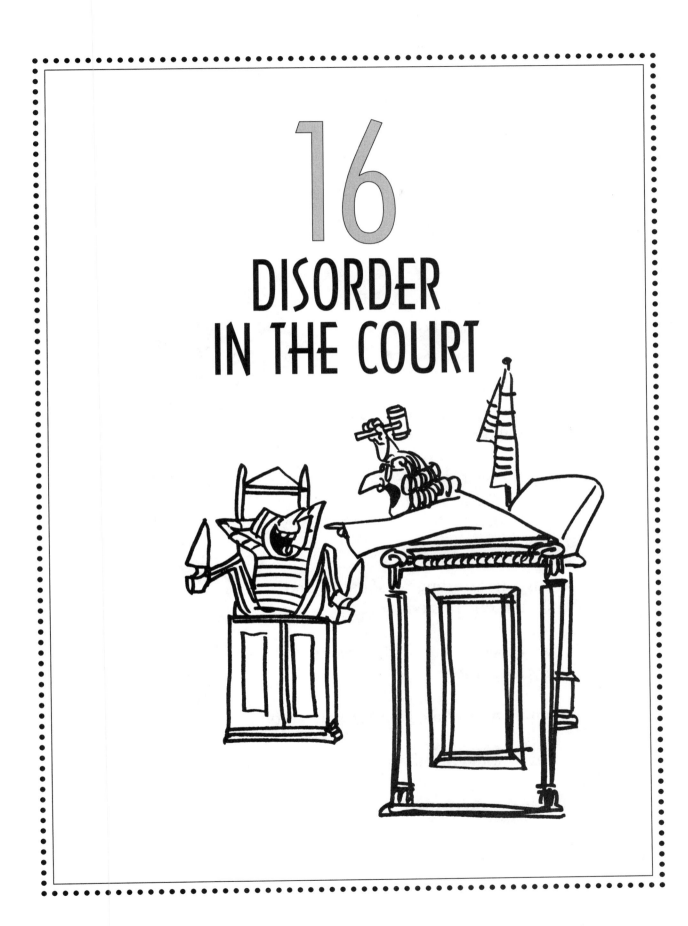

"Call out the narcotics squad—165 pounds of dope just walked in!"

You are wearing shoes to match your personality—sneakers.

You have a mind like a streak of lightning—
fast and crooked.

You're so crooked, you have
to screw your head on every
morning.

You're not a juvenile delinquent—
just an active, precocious young
person with homicidal tendencies.

If I were in your shoes—I'd shine them.

I've got to hand it to you, you're always trying—
very trying.

You have an arresting personality, and
you should be arrested for it.

The only time you're on the level is
when you're asleep.

I hear they named a cake after you—crumb.

You have more crust than a whole pie factory.

You're like a railroad train—plain loco and no motive.

Why be disagreeable? With a little more effort, you could be a real stinker.

You should work for the post office—even your brain is cancelled.

Where did you get your brains—at the bird store?

You've been in hot water so much, you look like a teabag.

You've been in more hot water than a boiled egg.

You'd be a real charmer if it weren't for your personality.

You're a real gyp off the old block.

You've been in so many jams, you could be spread on bread.

What you need is a pat on the back—often enough and low enough.

What does your mother do for a headache—send you out to play?

You have a fine mind, and anyone with a mind like yours should be fined.

Don't think it hasn't been pleasant knowing you — because it hasn't!

You never tell a lie when the truth will do more damage.

Make like scissors and cut out!

You have more nerve than an infected tooth.

The only regular exercise you get is stretching the truth.

You can't even tell the truth without lying.

Remember the fish—if he kept his mouth closed, he wouldn't get caught.

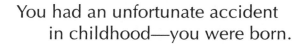

You had an unfortunate accident
in childhood—you were born.

Does the U.N. know about your face?
It looks like an undeclared war.

You're nobody's fool, but maybe
I can get someone to adopt you.

You started at the bottom—
and stayed there.

I know twelve people who would
like to meet you—a jury.

You're such a klutz, if you threw
yourself on the floor, you'd miss.

I'd like to hear your opinion, but isn't there enough
ignorance in the world already?

You remind me of someone important in history: the rear
end of what Paul Revere rode on.

You don't want anyone to make a fuss over you—just to
treat you as they would any celebrity.

I think you're the greatest, but then again, what do I know?

17
WHAT'S UP, DUCK?

Have I met you someplace before?
I sometimes get careless where I go.

If I had a face like yours, I'd walk
backwards.

You have a face that looks like it wore
out six bodies.

I never forget a face—but in your
case, I'll make an exception.

Your head is getting too big
for your toupee.

You're so conceited, you'd
join the navy so the world could
see you.

I don't care what anyone says,
I'll still talk to you.

You remind me of the ocean.
You never dry up.

Stupid? I hear you even flunked recess.

Wipe your nose. Your brains are leaking!

Your brain has paused permanently for station identification.

You're as strong as an ox—and just about as intelligent.

You had to become the outdoor type. No one would let you inside.

You really have a head on your shoulders. Too bad it's on backwards.

I hear you went to see a lot of doctors to have your head examined, but they couldn't find anything.

The more I think of you, the less I think of you.

Don't worry about losing your mind. You'd never miss it.

Where have you been all my life—and when are you going back there?

You think you're a great traveller just because your mind is always wandering.

Travel broadens a person. You look like you've been all over the world.

I'd like to make a complaint about you, but I don't feel like standing in line.

Your name must be Bob—spelled with two *o*'s.

You made a big mistake today. You got out of bed.

You remind me of a retired postman—no zip.

I hear you were a sickly baby. Did you live?

I hear you were a beautiful baby. What happened?

Is that a recent condition or were you born that way?

I've enjoyed talking to you. My mind needed the rest.

Why don't you make like a banana and split?

Things could be worse. You could be twins.

Don't give up. They'll find a cure for what's bothering you someday.

If I gave you a Kleenex, would you blow?

You're a perfect M.C.— (Mental Case).

You have low voice and a mentality to match.

Why don't you let your hair grow— right over your face?

Just because you dribble all over yourself doesn't make you a basketball player.

You must have a large brain to hold so much ignorance.

Next time you give away your old clothes—stay in them.

Don't go away. I want to forget you exactly as you are.

18
SQUEAK UP!

Are you a man or a mouse? Squeak up!

You're about as entertaining as one wrestler.

How did you get here, wriggle off the hook?

You're about as funny as an infected toenail.

You think you're a comedian, but you ought to be gagged.

I hear you were born on April 2nd—one day late.

You're so funny, I can hardly keep from not laughing.

Jokes like that will make humor illegal.

Even your jokes about old jokes are old.

You think you're funny, but you're only laughable.

I just contributed to a charity that might help you—the Mental Health Fund.

No wonder your mind is clear. It's not cluttered up with facts.

May I borrow your I.Q.? I'm going out with a moron tonight.

Your jokes are so corny, they could feed 200 chickens for five years.

You have a great future as a comedian. One look at you is enough to break anyone up.

You think you're a wit? Well, you're half right.

I like what you're wearing, but aren't you a little early (late) for Halloween?

I'd tell you to stop acting like a fool—but I don't think you're acting.

You made that joke up all by yourself out of your head? You must be!

I hope you live to be as
old as your jokes.

You remind me of a chicken—
always laying eggs.

If Adam came back to earth, the only
things he would recognize are your jokes.

You have a contagious laugh. People
get sick when they hear it.

Just keep on talking, so I'll know
what you're not thinking.

The last time I saw something like you, I pinned a tail on it.

I refuse to engage you in a battle of wits. I don't take
advantage of the handicapped.

Why don't you sit down and take a mess off your feet?

Don't sit down too hard. You could give yourself a brain
concussion.

You're out of this world and I hope you'll stay there.

You have a mechanical mind? Too bad it's never been wound up.

Don't go to a mind reader, go to a palmist. At least you know you've got a palm.

How would you like to be the first person to be kicked into orbit?

Stop looking in the mirror. Haven't you ever seen a moron before?

You have a ready wit. Please let me know when it's ready.

The only thing bright about you is the seat of your pants.

I guess you're okay when people get to know you. But who wants to get to know you?

If your mouth were any bigger, you could talk into your ears.

If you bit your tongue, you'd die of acid poisoning.

What a snob! You go out in the garden so the flowers can smell you.

Please play the guitar and stop picking on me.

Can I borrow your head for my rock garden?

What are you going to be—
if the neighbors let you grow up?

Who do I think I'm talking to?
How many guesses do I get?

When you get back home, give my regards to the warden.

When I want your opinion, I'll rattle your cage.

I can take a joke pretty far. Where do you want to go?

19
HELLO, HOT LIPS!

You should have been born in the
Dark Ages. You look awful in the light.

I could say nice things
about you, but I'd
rather tell the truth.

You have a striking
personality. How long
has it been on strike?

You'd make a good photographer—
the way you snap at people.

There's only one thing wrong with
your face—it's on the wrong end.

You can improve the quality of this conversation by keeping
your mouth shut.

You're probably not as dumb as you look. You couldn't be.

Is that your face or is today Halloween?

I don't know what I'd do without you. It's fun thinking
about it.

Surprise me. Say something intelligent.

Why don't you go to an antique store? Maybe someone
will buy you.

Why don't you make like a tree and leave?

You have the face of a saint— a Saint Bernard.

You have a face that looks better from the back.

You have that far-away look. The farther you get, the better you look.

You know, with the proper amount of coaching, you could be a nobody.

Please let me say goodbye until we never meet again.

You don't know the meaning of the word fear. You're too scared to look it up.

Your personality is so repulsive, even an echo wouldn't answer you.

If you have someplace to go—go!

I hope you never feel the way you look.

You'd make a perfect stranger.

Help improve the neighborhood—move!

Your visit has climaxed an already dull day.

You're not yourself today. I noticed the improvement right away.

I admit that you're stronger than I am, but bad breath isn't everything.

You have a lovely color in your cheeks—green.

Please don't change. Stay as stupid as you are.

You couldn't count to twenty without taking your shoes off.

Some people can tear a telephone book in half. You'd have trouble with a wet Kleenex.

You're in such bad shape, you couldn't jump to a conclusion.

You're so weak, you couldn't bend a wet noodle.

You're so weak, you couldn't even crack a joke.

The closest you'll ever get to being brave is to eat a hero sandwich.

You're in such bad shape, you'd have trouble beating a rug.

You're in such bad shape, you couldn't clear your throat.

You're such a coward, you're afraid to strike a bargain.

You're such a coward, you won't even strike a match.

Don't feel worthless. You can always be used as a horrible example.

Two is company. You're a crowd.

Want to see something funny? Look in the mirror.

Of course, you're not a coward. You just have a low threshold of pain.

I've heard so much about you. What's your side of the story?

You're not a coward. You just can't stand the sight of blood—yours.

When you sing it reminds me of pirates—murder on the high C's.

We have a cow on the farm that makes noises like you, but it also gives milk.

You have a good voice—if you don't happen to like music.

When you sing people clap their hands—over their ears.

Of course your voice is pure. Every time you sing, you strain it.

Singers run in your family—and they should.

I've heard better sounds come from a leaking balloon.

Your voice reminds me of water being let out of a tub.

The best way to improve your face is to keep the lower half shut.

You throw yourself into everything you do? Please go out and dig a deep hole!

Your brain is so weak, you have to wear crutches under your ears.

Please make like a bee and buzz off!

Next time you pass my house—pass my house.

At least you're original. You make a new mistake every day.

You're a natural musician. Your tongue is sharp and your feet are flat.

I wish you were on TV so I could turn you off.

Your voice is as flat as your head.

Your voice reminds me of a machine at home that sucks up dirt.

You couldn't carry a tune if it had a handle.

I love music—but please keep on singing anyway.

You say you sing with feeling. If you had any feeling, you wouldn't sing.

Your voice is heavenly—I mean, unearthly.

Do you know
"The Road to Mandalay?"
I don't mean sing it—
I mean take it.

You sing like a bird and
have a brain to match.

Anyone with a voice
like yours ought to be
arrested for disturbing
the peace.

Signal when you're
finished singing, so I
can take my fingers out
of my ears.

You do your singing in the
shower? Don't sing very often,
do you?

You could make a living hiring yourself out as a noisemaker at parties.

You could make a living souring milk.

139

You're the flower of manhood—
a blooming idiot.

Dracula would turn you
down. He wants plasma,
not asthma.

You sing like a bird—a cuckoo.

Your mouth is so
big, you can sing
duets all by yourself.

After they made
you, they broke the
jelly mold.

The muscles in your arms are
like potatoes—mashed potatoes.

You look pretty today—pretty awful.

You always seem to mind your business
at the top of your lungs.

You have a fine voice. Don't spoil it by singing.

You sound much better with your mouth closed.

I'd like to rock you to sleep—with big ones.

140

If I ever want to remember
your voice, I just tear a rag.

Your voice is too loud for
indoor use.

You missed being
Miss America by two feet:
twelve inches on each hip.

21
THE GREAT DEBATE

Is that your head, or did somebody find a way to grow hair on a meatball?

You may be thoughtless—but you're never speechless.

You may be outspoken, but I can't think of by whom.

Generally speaking—
you're generally speaking.

You're someone who never
goes without saying.

You're like a tugboat—
the more you're in a fog,
the louder you toot.

Better to keep your mouth shut
and let people suspect that you're
stupid, than to open it and remove
all doubt.

The only thing you ever exercise
is your tongue.

You have a tongue that would
clip a hedge.

Your tongue is always sticking
out, so why can't you hold it?

You use your tongue so much, you need a retread every six months.

Your tongue is so long, you can seal an envelope after you put it in the mailbox.

Your tongue is so long, when it hangs out, people think it's your tie.

I like the straightforward way you dodge the issues.

You never let the facts interfere with your opinions.

You have nothing to say, but that doesn't stop you from saying it.

You talk so much I get hoarse just listening to you.

You never learned to swim. You couldn't keep your mouth closed long enough.

Success hasn't gone to your head, only to your mouth.

Please turn off your mouth. It's still running.

You should try to get ahead. You could certainly use one.

Next to your head, the biggest bones in your body are your jaws.

Please close your mouth so I can see the rest of your face.

You have so much bridgework, anyone who kissed you would have to pay a toll.

You talk so much, even your tonsils get tired.

You could make a fortune by hiring yourself out to fill hot air balloons.

You ought to be on the Parole Board. You never let anyone finish a sentence.

Your main trouble is that you never make a long story short.

I didn't say you had a big mouth, only that I saw you bobbing for basketballs.

Your mind may be slow, but your mouth is fast.

You're the talk of the town—all by yourself.

We can always depend on you to start the bull rolling.

You're so full of bull, the cows must follow you home.

Chickens must like you because you're such a big cluck.

You're a person of few words—
a few million words.

Help prevent air pollution.
Stop talking!

You couldn't tell which way the
elevator was going if you had
two guesses.

I liked you when we first met,
but you talked me out of it.

If after a reasonable time your speech
doesn't strike oil, you'd better stop boring.

Please close your mouth. It's getting
hot in here.

You're the sleeping pill of the
speaking profession.

You're not boring me. Just wake me up when you're finished talking.

You're such a bore. You won't change your mind—or the subject.

You're such a bore, even my leg falls asleep when you talk.

You always speak straight from the shoulder—too bad your words don't start from higher up.

I've heard better conversations in alphabet soup.

Your ideas are so corny, they'd sound better with butter and salt.

If baloney were snow, you'd be a blizzard.

Some people can speak on any subject. You don't need a subject.

A brain isn't everything. In your case, it's nothing.

You have a point there—your head!

I have a minute to spare—tell me everything you know.

There are two sides to every question—and you always take both.

You're the decisive type. You'll always give a definite maybe.

Your speech reminds me of the horns of a steer—
a point here and there, and a lot of bull
in between.

Just because you have a hole
in your head doesn't mean
you have an open mind.

22
MAN OVERBOARD!

If they ever put a price on your head—take it!

You're not really such a bad person—until people get to know you.

I've seen large windows, but you're the biggest pain of them all.

Just because you have a sunken chest doesn't make you a treasure.

If you stepped out to visit all your friends, you'd be back in a minute.

You have a heart of gold—yellow and hard.

You certainly have a nice personality. I think all your friends are wrong.

Quick, get a hammer! There's a fly on your head.

If you've got no place to go, I could suggest one.

What do you do for a living? You are living, aren't you?

You're perfect for hot weather. You leave me cold.

I'd like to see you in something flowing. Why don't you jump in the river?

Do you still love Mother Nature—in spite of what she did to you?

If you had your life to live over—would you please do it somewhere else?

You're so stingy, you won't even pay attention.

151

No wonder your brain is good as new. It's never been used.

If you're such a treasure, where did they dig you up?

You have ears like a shovel—always picking up dirt.

The only thing you should fear more than losing your mind is finding it.

You don't need to wear jewelry. You already have enough rings under your eyes.

I'd like to buy you two things for your neck— soap and rope.

If you won't have your hair cut, at least change the oil.

You're such a coward, you wouldn't even fight temptation.

You're such a coward, you'd be afraid to strike a pose.

You were such a homely baby, your parents sent you back and kept the stork.

I'd like to give you
something you need,
but I don't know
how to wrap up a bathtub.

You're a heel without a soul.

The only things that can stand getting close to you are fleas.

If I don't get in touch with you in a year or two, please show me the same consideration.

Are you really leaving, or are you just trying to brighten my day?

23
YOU WORM, YOU!

When I watch you eat, I know where they got the idea for "Jaws."

I think of you often. But I'd rather not say what.

You must be sick. That can't be your natural appearance.

I was feeling fine until you came along.

I hear you won the King Kong look-alike contest.

You know the old gag, "Your face would stop a clock?" Well, yours would stop a sundial.

You're like medicine— hard to swallow.

You look like a nervous wreck. Okay, so you're not nervous.

What's wrong with you? How about if I gave it to you alphabetically?

You're so weak, you couldn't even carry a tune.

You're so weak, you couldn't even bat an eyelash.

You're so weak,
you couldn't even lick a lollipop.

If you tried to whip cream, the cream would win.

If you wore stilts, you'd still be a midget.

You're so short, when it rains you're the last one to know.

You're so short, you can pole vault with a toothpick.

You're so small, I couldn't even wipe my feet on you.

You're so small that when you take a bath, you have to wear snowshoes to keep from going down the drain.

Good things may come in small packages, but so does poison.

Didn't I see you once before under a microscope?

You're so short, you can't tell if you have a headache or your corns hurt.

You're so short, you play handball against the curb.

There's something about you I like. Give me a year or two, I'll remember it.

If I gave you a going-away present—would you?

157

24
SPEAK UP, DUMMY!

If there was an Olympics for stupidity, you'd break all records.

You were born with a big handicap—your mouth.

You remind me of decaffeinated coffee—no active ingredient in the bean.

You should wear a soft hat—to match your head.

You don't look well. When was the last time you saw your veterinarian?

I finally figured out what's eating you— termites.

I hear your family were the early Boones— the Baboons.

The only time you make sense is when you're not talking.

If a bird had your brain it would fly backwards.

The only thing your head is good for is to keep your ears apart.

Why don't you send your mind to the laundry?

If it weren't for your stupidity, you wouldn't have any personality at all.

Your ears are bookends for a vacuum.

That's a nice outfit you're wearing. Didn't they have it in your size?

What's the matter? Didn't you like the food they gave you in the zoo?

You must have a clean mind— you change it so often.

You never change your mind? No wonder—no mind.

Know how to earn extra money? Rent out your head. It's empty anyhow!

Didn't I see you hanging around the faucet, you big drip?

Who wears your *good* clothes?

Now I know why you smile all the time. Your teeth are the only things about you that aren't wrinkled.

Does the undertaker know you're up?

I don't believe in talking to strangers—and you're the strangest person I ever saw.

Don't worry if your mind wanders. It's too weak to go very far.

In your case, an ounce of keep-your-mouth shut beats a pound of talking.

You say you have a mind of your own? Why don't you bring it around some time?

Do it tomorrow. You've made enough mistakes today.

You're so short, you have to wear socks to keep your neck warm.

You're so short, if you pulled your socks up, you'd be blindfolded.

You're not prejudiced. You hate everybody regardless of race, color or creed.

Use your head. It's the little things that count.

Why don't you deprive me of your company for a few years?

Your idea of a big evening is to take out the garbage.

You're so cheap, you even have your garbage gift wrapped.

The only thing you ever give away is secrets.

Of course I'm listening to you. Don't you see me yawning?

25
TOOTH OR CONSEQUENCES

You may become famous in history—
medical history!

They should cover you with
chocolate, because you're
nuts!

You're a real life saver.
I can tell by the hole in
your head.

Whatever is eating you
must be suffering from food
poisoning.

When your grandfather was born,
they passed out cigars. When your
father was born, they passed out
cigarettes. When you were born, they
just passed out.

When you were born, your parents looked up your birth
certificate to see if there were any loopholes in it.

You're a chip off the old block—a real blockhead.

What you lack in looks, you make up for in stupidity.

Keep talking. Maybe you'll find something to say one day.

They don't make money in small enough denominations to
pay you what you're worth.

You're just what the doctor ordered—a pill!

Where did you find your mind—in the gutter?

Do you have a license to drive people crazy?

You're not hard of hearing, just hard of listening.

Your remarks may be pointless, but not your head.

Have you been to the zoo lately? I mean, as a visitor?

Stay with me—I want to be alone.

Is that dandruff on your shoulders or sawdust leaking out of your ears?

Why don't you make like dandruff and flake off?

Close your mouth before someone puts an apple in it.

Don't try to diet. There's no way to reduce a fat head.

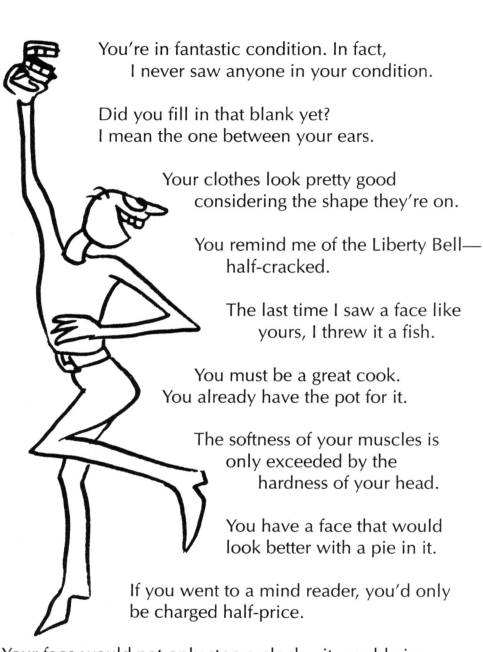

You're in fantastic condition. In fact,
I never saw anyone in your condition.

Did you fill in that blank yet?
I mean the one between your ears.

Your clothes look pretty good
considering the shape they're on.

You remind me of the Liberty Bell—
half-cracked.

The last time I saw a face like
yours, I threw it a fish.

You must be a great cook.
You already have the pot for it.

The softness of your muscles is
only exceeded by the
hardness of your head.

You have a face that would
look better with a pie in it.

If you went to a mind reader, you'd only
be charged half-price.

Your face would not only stop a clock—it would give
Father Time a heart attack.

Even people who don't know you don't like you.

166

You look like you had an argument with a freight train—
and lost.

Everyone says you're a silly ass, but I don't think you're
silly.

You're so narrow-minded, you can look through a keyhole
with both eyes.

You may be high-strung, but not high enough to suit me.

Why don't you leave your brain to science? Maybe they
can find a cure for it.

You could make a fortune helping people lose weight. One
look at you and people lose their appetite.

Most of us live and learn—
you just live.

I've got something in my
eye that's painful—you.

Beauty isn't everything.
In your case, it's nothing.

Don't worry about anyone
making a monkey out of you.
Nature did it already.

Please make like a ball and roll
away!

Remember, he who thinks by the inch and talks by the yard
—deserves to be kicked by the foot.

No wonder you've never been kissed—
your mouth has never been still
 long enough.

If you need me—hesitate to call.

26
OH, WHAT BIG EYES YOU HAVE!

Your eyes are like pools—sunken and watery.

Your lips remind me of petals—bicycle pedals.

You have calves that only a cow would like.

You may be as fit as a fiddle, but you look more like a saxophone to me.

If you went to the beauty parlor, they wouldn't let you in.

You must be older than you look. No one could get so dumb so fast.

I'm dumb? You spent two weeks in a revolving door looking for a doorknob.

You couldn't win a beauty contest if there were no other contestants.

You have a soft heart and a head to match.

You're not yourself today—thank goodness!

If you had a face, I wouldn't like it either.

You have an hourglass figure, but the sand has settled in the wrong place.

You have a schoolgirl figure, but it looks like it played hooky.

You're looks aren't half-bad. They're all bad.

Last night I dreamed I saw something in front of your house that made me very happy—a moving van.

Your face reminds me of a flower—a cauliflower.

Are you always so stupid or is today a special occasion?

Every time I pass a garbage pail, I think of you.

Please close your mouth, there's an awful draft in here.

What happened at your coming-out party, did they make you go back in?

You'd make a perfect model—for a dumbbell.

You should be in the movies. You look better in the dark.

Do you go to school to learn to be so stupid, or does it come naturally?

You dress well for someone who is obviously color-blind.

You don't have enough sense to pull your head in when you shut the window.

The only thing that would whistle at you is a steam kettle.

You have a pretty little head. And for a head, it's pretty little.

That dress fits you like a glove. Too bad it doesn't fit you like a dress.

Why don't you go to a pet shop? Maybe someone will buy you.

Is that your face, or are you breaking it in for Dr. Frankenstein?

27
WANT TO EAT OUT?

What's on the plate, in case I have to describe it to my doctor?

You're so fond of arguing, you wouldn't eat anything that agreed with you.

What's on your mind—if you'll forgive the exaggeration.

You're bright and early—well, at least, early.

The only quick thing about you is your watch.

The only thing you do fast is get tired.

Of course I enjoyed the cooking.
Do you have a stomach pump handy?

Keep your words soft and sweet.
You never know when you might have to eat them.

I'm now convinced it is possible to communicate with the dead.
I can hear you distinctly.

You're not only wet behind the ears—you're all wet.

Why don't you stand up and give your brain a rest?

I'd like to tell you how I feel about you, but not while I'm eating.

Better hide, I see the garbage collector coming.

It's not the ups and downs in life that bother me, but the jerks like you.

You wouldn't say that if you were conscious.

The next time you wash your neck, wring it.

I know a perfect restaurant for you.
They serve soup to nuts.

You must be on a sea food diet. You eat all the food you can see.

Are those your feet, or are you breaking them in for a duck?

You must be an actor. You're so good at making scenes.

Don't complain about the coffee. You may be old and weak yourself some day.

You're so lazy, you wait for the wind to blow your nose.

You're the perfect cure for anyone with an inferiority complex.

You're so tired at the end of the day, I bet you can hardly keep your mouth open.

Tell me, is your family happy— or do you still live at home?

You may be your own worst enemy—but not when I'm around.

I hear your friends threw you a big dinner. Too bad it missed.

Your face looks like you slept in it.

Your kitchen is famous. It's the place where flies come to commit suicide.

There is nothing wrong with you that a brain transplant couldn't cure.

They put brighter heads than yours on matchsticks.

Your cooking would be fine if I were a termite.

You have a big mouth—and an appetite to match.

Even your TV-Dinners are re-runs.

You not only don't know how to cook, you don't know what's cooking.

You must be a Minute Man—the way you stuff yourself. You've already had sixty seconds!

You really are cooking with gas. How about inhaling some?

You'd make a great football player. Even your breath is offensive.

Listen to you eat. You sound like a soup-rano.

You eat like a bird—a vulture!

Why don't you go on a diet and quit eating my heart out?

No one can stand you—but that's your only fault.

I could break you in half, but who would want two of you?

It would take you five minutes to boil a three-minute egg.

You may aim to please, but you're a terrible shot.

There are two reasons why you don't mind your own business—(1) no mind—(2) no business.

A little bird whispered something in your ear. It must have been a cuckoo.

Know how to lose ten ugly pounds? Cut your head off!

Where were you when brains were handed out?

What are you *not* thinking about now?

Does the Board of Health know you're running around loose?

If you must know, I'm ignoring you.

Don't go away mad—just go away!

As guests go, I wish you would.

28
YOU'RE STANDING ON MY FOOT!

Is that a new hairdo or did you just walk through a wind tunnel?

The person who said all things must end never heard you talk.

You're so pale, the only way you get color in your face is to stick your tongue out.

Were your parents disappointed? They must have wanted children.

The only time people treat you with respect is during "Be Kind To Dumb Animals Week."

You don't need much makeup. You have plenty of color from the diaper rash on your face.

Please breathe the other way. You're bleaching my hair.

Tell me, did any children in your family live?

What would you say if I told you I had a bright idea?
    "Nothing. I can't talk and laugh at the same time."

I hear they're making a study of your family tree. You must be the sap.

Please follow the example of your head and come to the point.

Look, if you want to argue with me, I'll go out and check my brains, so we can start even.

Some figures stop traffic. Yours only blocks it.

You are smarter than you look, but then again, you'd have to be.

You pick your friends—
to pieces.

You had such a pretty chin, you decided to add two more.

You have so many chins, you need a bookmark to find your collar.

Your ideas are like diamonds—
very rare.

Don't feel bad if you have a cold in your head. At least that's something.

You have a schoolgirl complexion. It looks like it was expelled.

No mind reader could read your mind. The print is too small.

Having trouble making up what's left of your mind?

You have a figure like an hourglass. It takes an hour to figure it out.

You look like Monroe— not the actress, the President.

You have lips like cherries— and a nose to match.

The closest you'll ever come to being a classy dish is owning a set of china.

That's some perfume you're wearing. Who sold it to you, a skunk?

When you go to the zoo, I hear the monkeys throw peanuts at you.

You don't know the meaning of the word "fear"—besides the thousands of other words you don't know the meaning of.

You have a memory like an elephant and a shape to match.

You remind me of a banana without its skin—no appeal.

Oh, you're walking today! Did someone hide the broomstick?

You had an idea once, but it died of loneliness.

Your clothes match your mouth. They're both loud.

Isn't it a shame you can t get anyone to love you the way you love yourself?

Dreamboat? You're more like a shipwreck.

The only big thing about you is your opinion of yourself.

You're so conceited, I hear you have your X-rays retouched.

Your idea of a real treat is to stand in front of the mirror and look at yourself.

You've known only one great love in your life—you.

You always walk with your nose in the air—that's to avoid smelling yourself.

Just what is it that you see in you?

Either your dress is too short, or you're in it too far.

You have hidden talents—well hidden.

You bought those clothes for a ridiculous figure—yours.

When you were poured into your clothes, you forgot to say "when."

You swim like a duck and have a shape to match.

The only thing that you can keep in your head is a cold.

The only tense you use in speaking is pretense.

You're more than touchy—you're touched!

Tell me, when you go to the zoo, do the animals recognize you?

If ignorance is bliss, you must be the happiest person on earth.

Those words must come from your heart. They certainly don't come from your brain.

You're always sincere—whether you mean it or not.

If your I.Q. were any lower, you'd trip over it.

I don't know what I'd do without you, but I'd rather.

I'm sorry you didn't like my telling people you were stupid. I had no idea it was a secret.

Lazy? Your idea of cleaning house is to sit in a corner and collect dust.

Just because you are always harping on things doesn't make you an angel.

I understand that at Christmas they hang you up and kiss the mistletoe.

I think you're wonderful. But what is my opinion against millions of others?

Just because you're always exploding doesn't make you a big shot.

Look at you! Was anyone else hurt in the accident?

29
SCHOOL—GO SLOW

Why did you bring your dog in here?

Shh—this is my cat. He only thinks he's my dog.

What's that on your desk?

Nuclear fallout.

An abstract replica of Mount Everest.

Recycled spitballs from the Environment Committee.

A food sample from the cafeteria I'm analyzing for science class.

Why are you writing with your left hand when you told me you're a rightie?

I was writing a left-handed compliment.

I screwed my arms on backwards this morning.

I wasn't in the right mood.

I woke up on the wrong side of the bed.

Why don't you ever pay attention?

I did once and it wouldn't pay me back.

It doesn't take credit cards.

I never got a bill.

How much do I have to pay it?

Why do you always daydream during math?

That isn't daydreaming! It's a post-hypnotic trance.

Because I forgot to do it during social studies.

Is this math class? I thought it was still Penmanship.

I wasn't daydreaming. I was working a problem out in my head.

I wasn't daydreaming. I was having an out-of-body experience.

I'm doing geometry. I'm thinking about the Bermuda Triangle.

I'm doing arithmetic. I'm figuring out how many shopping days till Christmas.

What happened to your pencil?

This isn't a pencil. It's an overweight toothpick with a
   giant zit.

Oh, this is a Christmas present from my termite.

The pencil sharpener went into a feeding frenzy.

This isn't a pencil. It's petrified
   beef jerky.

30
CLASS COME TO ORDER!

Why do you always squeak the chalk?

I'm sending messages in Mouse Code.

Why are you writing on the blackboard?

Because I can't reach the ceiling.

'Cause I'm bored of education!

The paper isn't big enough to hold all my thoughts.

Because you told me not to write on the floor.

It's got more space than my notebook.

Why don't you answer my question?

Didn't you tell me not to answer back?

Did you ever hear of the Fifth Amendment?

I'm waiting for the multiple choice.

My answer is none of the above.

I'm saving my answers for *Jeopardy*.

Don't you ever stop talking?

Stop Talking? Stop it from what?

I'm not talking—I'm practising
    word-processing.

Well, talk is cheap and I can't
    afford anything better.

My lips keep coming unzipped.

Where's Talking going?

I had alphabet soup for lunch
    and words keep coming
    out of my mouth.

I don't know—
    I'm not listening.

Why are you calling out?

Would you prefer that I telephone?

I didn't know how to call in.

That was my inner voice
struggling to be heard.

I was an auctioneer in
a former life.

These shoes are new and
they're killing me.

It's cheaper than sending a
singing telegram.

Why are you raising your hand when I asked everyone to wait until I finished the story?

I'm not! I'm testing out my new deodorant.

I'm not! I'm drying my nail polish.

I'm not! I'm swatting flies.

I'm not! I'm hailing a cab.

I'm not! I'm unscrewing my arm.

I'm not! I'm clearing the air.

I'm not! I'm holding up the ceiling.

What are you doing crawling around the floor?

I wanted to get to the bottom of things.

Just getting down to the nitty-gritty.

I was actually crawling on the ceiling, but I fell off.

31
WHAT ARE YOU DOING?

Why aren't you folding your hands?

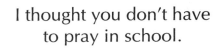

I thought you don't have
to pray in school.

I folded my paper.
Isn't that enough?

I thought it would count
if I just crossed my
fingers.

Why are you scribbling all over your desk?

I'm not. I'm writing neatly.

I'm not. I'm just adding my name to the list of other great people who sat here.

I'm not. I'm just answering some of the personals.

I ran out of paper.

I was following orders. Didn't you say, "Mark my word?"

Why are you standing on the desk?

I like to stay on top of things.

I'm above average in everything.

I was set up.

Because I don't know how to stand on my head.

I'm trying to upgrade my image.

I function on a very high level.

I'm preparing for a summit conference.

Why did you throw the paper airplane out the window?

I wanted to join the jet set.

You said to get rid of it.

I was giving my pet ant a free ride.

I was feeling space-y.

Because it doesn't have an automatic launcher.

I was testing a new way to do my paper route.

I was too tired to carry it home.

What paper airplane? That was Flight 905 to Daytona.

Why were you absent from school yesterday?

I wasn't absent. I was temporarily invisible.

Absence is my only A.

I wanted to see if the class could survive without me.

So the room wouldn't be overcrowded.

Because absence makes the heart grow fonder.

32
WHAT'S THE MATTER WITH YOU?

Did you get sunburned?

No—I'm just an unusually bright kid.

Why do you keep running around the room?

My nose is the only thing that's running. The rest of me is just trying to keep up.

I'm standing still. The room is running around me.

I'm practising for a career on the merry-go-round.

I'm part of the human race, aren't I?

I'm trying to find where it begins.

The doctor told me not to get run down.

Are you thirsty again?

No. I'm filling my waterbed.

No. I'm about to fill the swimming pool.

No. I'm Friday.

No, my room is on fire and I'm just going to put it out.

No, I'm going to take a bath.

Why are you putting on lipstick in class?

I'm getting ready for my make-up exam.

I'm trying to make it easy for my voice to find its way out of my mouth.

This is my ecology homework. I'm beautifying the environment.

Why did you push me?

Because you're a pushy kid.

I was too tired to pull you.

Because there wasn't anyone else around to push.

I thought you wanted to get ahead in life.

Why do you always pull my hair?

I like to get to the root of things.

Is that what it is—I thought it was linguine with clam sauce.

It's too hard to push it.

Just hunting for endangered species.

I'll stop—I don't want to upset the ecological balance.

I thought maybe your brush was stuck in there.

**Is that a new ring
on your finger?**

Yes, the one in the
    bathtub didn't fit.

No, it's a Cheerio.
    Got some milk?

No, it's a bracelet that shrank
    at the cleaners.

No, it's a lifesaver I'm saving
    for after lunch.

Why don't you listen when I talk to you?

I am listening. Don't you see me yawning?

Sorry—I thought your ventriloquist was doing the talking.

I can either listen to you talk or watch you dribble, but I can't do both.

Oh, excuse me—I thought you were talking in your sleep.

**Why are you showing off
your dimples?**

They're not dimples. I just had my face pierced.

Oh, they're just places where I hide my chewing gum.

What dimples? Those are inverted pimples.

33
WHY DID YOU DO IT?

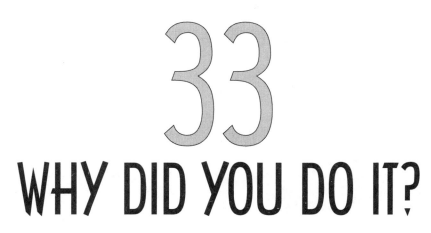

Did you tear your pants?

No, that's my built-in air conditioner.

Why did you get a zero on your test?

That's not a zero—
it's the 15th letter of the
alphabet. My teacher
couldn't remember the
other ones.

That's not a zero—
it's a moon. The
teacher ran out of stars.

That's not a zero—
it's a racetrack
for fleas.

That's not a zero—
it's a picture of
Cyclops' eye.

Why didn't you take the garbage out?

It's hard to dance with a Hefty bag.

It just wouldn't be home without it.

We're not interested in the same things.

It never takes me out.

I had another date.

Why didn't you go to the dentist?

Because he always chews me out.

Drills are boring!

I'm too attached to my teeth.

He always takes my gum.

The tooth fairy offered me a better deal.

I think children should be seen and not hurt.

Why didn't you see the doctor when you were supposed to?

Every time I see him my tongue gets depressed.

I did see him—but I don't remember where.

I saw him—Dr. Huxtable on TV!

Because he loses his patients.

'Cause he tells sick jokes.

What happened to your brains today?

The dentist drilled too deep.

I blew my nose too hard.

I was being brainwashed and they went down the drain.

34
WHAT'S NEW?

Are you gaining weight?

No, your eyes are just getting smaller.

No, you shrank my clothes.

That's a heavy
question.

Why do you still bite your nails?

My fingers are too long.

They taste better than nuts and bolts.

I'm on a high protein diet.

I don't.
    They just get worn down from scratching my head.

My toenails are too hard to reach.

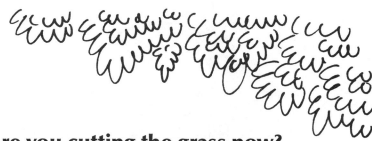

Are you cutting the grass now?

No, I'm feeding my pet lawn mower.

No, this is an outdoor vacuum cleaner.

Did you go to the supermarket again?

No, I'm walking my shopping cart.

No, all this food just came in
the mail.

Are you going swimming again?

No, just going to wash the lint out of my bellybutton.

No, I'm checking to see if the oysters I planted last year have grown any pearls.

No, I just want to find out if I have drip-dry skin.

No, I'm just getting ready for the swimsuit competition.

Are you going skiing?

No, I'm carrying chopsticks for the Jolly Green Giant.

No, I'm laying a railroad track.

No, these are just the rabbit ears for my new TV.

228

Is that a surfboard?

Surfboard? This is an ironing board for bikinis.

No, it's a starched beach blanket.

No, it's a tongue depressor
for my pet shark.

Is that a tennis racket?

No, this is my Abominable Snowshoe.

No, I use this to paddle my canoe.

No, this is a giant fly swatter.

Why did your baseball team lose?

The coach turned into a pumpkin.

We were way off base.

Everyone went batty.

35
EATING IT UP

Why are you hiccuping?

I'm not. This is an epiglottal seizure.

I just ate franks and Mexican
jumping beans.

I swallowed a beeper.

Why aren't you eating the school lunch?

I ate some of it last year, but now it's getting stale.

I'm waiting for the Board of Health to analyze it.

School lunch? I thought this was leftovers from chemistry class.

I take poison at home, thank you.

I left my gas mask at home.

Why are you eating with your fingers?

Would you rather I ate with your fingers?

It's neater than eating with my toes.

It beats eating with my elbows.

I tried eating with my baseball mitt, but I couldn't get the food into my mouth.

'Cause I'm hungry.

I'm not. I'm putting my fingers in my mouth.

Can you imagine eating without them?

Do you always keep your elbows on the table?

No. but you never know when you'll meet an Indian wrestler.

No, I was holding up my chin.

No, I was just afraid the lunch tray was going to blow away.

Yes, I try to be symmetrical.

No, sometimes I keep them in a big box.

Only when I'm eating them with tomato sauce.

Is the food too spicy?

No, smoke always comes out of my ears.

No, but I think my hair has just become naturally curly.

I'll tell you when I stop crying.

36
HEY, YOU!

Why aren't you with your class?

That's classified information.

I'm in a class
   by myself.

Is that my kite?

No—it's a stingray on a leash.

No, I'm trying to catch a flying fish.

No, I'm just drying my laundry piece by piece.

Why are you such a big pest?

I started out being a little pest, but practice makes perfect.

Am I really a pest? I was trying to be more of a general
nuisance.

Sheer talent, I guess!

It's my mother's fault. She called the exterminator but I was
outside playing.

Why are you wearing glasses?

I use these hooks to keep my face attached to the rest of my head.

I have to. They keep my eyeballs from falling out

I'm planning to do some sightseeing.

I like making a spectacle of myself.

Why are you standing on your head?

Would you rather I stand on
your head?

I'm trying to get the dustballs
out of my pockets.

That's funny. I thought it was the room
that was upside down.

Because your head is too far
off the ground.

I'm giving my brains a workout.

241

You call that playing basketball?

No, I always dribble after lunch.

No, actually I thought I was doing the backstroke.

No, baseball.
Isn't that home plate up there on the backboard?

No, I'm checking the ceiling for cobwebs.

No, I thought I was playing golf, but I can't find the first hole.

Why are you always fighting?

I'm wrestling with that question.

It must be these boxer shorts I'm wearing.

Beats me.

37
GO TO YOUR ROOM!

Are you sneezing?

No, this is how we say
"Hello" in Martian.

Why are your clothes all wet?

The label says wash and wear.

I ran out of quarters for the dryer.

I just finished walking
my pet fish.

I'm wishy-washy.

I didn't fit in the dryer.

Why didn't you close the door?

There's a mosquito in here with claustrophobia.

Because we're such a close-knit family.

I'm expecting a friend who knows too many knock-knocks.

Because I have an open mind.

I'm waiting for Santa Claus.

Because there's a sabre-tooth tiger in the house.

Because my poltergeist would get lonely.

What's this candy doing in your bed?

Don't ask me. I gave it a good licking and sent it home.

I wanted to have sweet dreams.

It's not candy. It's medicine for my sweet tooth.

Getting a little bit of rest.

That's a sticky subject.

I thought it was a tasteful decoration.

Why don't you make your bed?

And disturb all the crumbs?

The dog's still in it.

I'm not a carpenter.

Why are your toys all over the floor?

I don't know. It must be some kind of convention.

Roger Rabbit must be casting his next movie.

Ask them. I told them to
    stay in their box.

They're all wound up.

A toynado hit them.

Why don't you turn off the lights?

I was trying to trap a killer moth.

I'm conserving solar energy.

The last time I turned off the light, I couldn't find the way out.

I'd only have to turn them on again.

I didn't want to wear out the switch.

Didn't you tell me you invested in energy stocks?

You got me. I'm completely in the dark.

I'm a light sleeper.

Watt?

Why don't you clean your room?

My room? I thought it was my closet.

Mr. Clean was always cleaning his room and what did he get to show for it but a bald head?

I did clean it. It just got dirty again.

Because it's not Leap Year.

We ran out of Kleenex.

I couldn't find it.

INDEX